D1824093

Now I can . . .

Spell

Brown Book

By Ronald Ridout

Illustrated by Colin Caket

Collins
in association with
 Belitha Press

Dear Adult,

May I tell you briefly what the essence of NOW I CAN
SPELL is?

First, it consists of eight graded write-in books to help young
beginners over the first steps of learning to spell.

The first book (Pink) begins with words of one syllable, but
always with their meaning made clear by pictures. By the last
book (Brown), children are spelling words of two syllables.

Children will neither make much progress, nor have the
encouragement to go on trying, unless they can do the spelling.
NOW I CAN SPELL is, therefore, completely self-guided
throughout. The children are enabled to do the spelling on their
own, and very largely without mistakes, because the means to
come to the right answer is always available.

NOW I CAN SPELL is specially suited to young children
working at home, as it is the most gradual and the most helpful
learning-to-spell series there has ever been.

I am sure with this book and your help your child will make the
maximum progress in learning to spell.

Yours sincerely,

Ronald Ridout

First published 1985 by Collins Educational, London and Glasgow
in association with Belitha Press Limited,
31 Newington Green, London N16 9PU
Reprinted 1986   Revised edition published by William Collins Sons and Co Ltd 1987
Text and illustrations in this format copyright © Belitha Press 1985, 1987
Text copyright © Ronald Ridout 1985
Illustrations copyright © the estate of Colin Caket 1985
All rights reserved. No part of this publication may be reproduced
in any form whatsoever without the permission of
the publishers and the copyright holders.
ISBN 0 00 197435 1
Typesetting by Chambers Wallace, London
Printed by Purnell Book Production Limited Paulton, England

Write these words under the pictures, and then put them in the right boxes.

owls   horses   turkeys
wasps   parrots   flies
mice   lions   beetles

_ _ _ _ _ _ _

_ _ _ _ _ _ _

_ _ _ _ _ _ _

_ _ _ _ _ _ _

_ _ _ _ _ _ _

_ _ _ _ _ _ _

_ _ _ _ _ _ _

_ _ _ _ _ _ _

_ _ _ _ _ _ _

These have two legs

These have four legs

These have six legs

A Write the complete words, like this:

h f w tipt	
toe	toe
– oe	hoe
– oe	
– oe	
– – – – oe	

m st wh fem	
pale	
– ale	
– – ale	
– – ale	
– – – ale	

r m sh sc	
care	
– are	
– are	
– – are	
– – are	

B l sn kn	
hobby	
– obby	
– obby	
– – obby	
– – obby	

B Find the words to write under these pictures.

Bobby

_ _ _ _ _

_ _ _ _ _ _

_ _ _ _ _

_ _ _ _

_ _ _ _ _ _

4

A Put the right names on my labels.

Arm	Leg
wrist	ankle
fingers	knee
palm	calf
elbow	toes
thumb	heel

B Write the whole words:

1. el + bow =

2. fin + ger =

3. ank + le =

4. simp + le =

5. rain + bow =

6. ti + ger =

7. an + ger =

8. shoul + der =

A Write the complete words, like this:

da ic sy ther	
pant	pant
pan – –	panda
pan – –	
pan – –	
pan – – – –	

ng per fit verb	
prop	
pro – –	
pro – – –	
pro – – –	
pro – – – –	

ch bal rom dist	
dance	
– – ance	
– – – ance	
– – – ance	
– – – – ance	

ac doc visi trac	
motor	
– – tor	
– – – tor	
– – – – tor	
– – – – tor	

B Now put the right name under each of these pictures.

Make the complete words:

her		1. _____
him		2. _____
it	self	3. _____
my		4. _____
your		5. _____

 Now use the words to finish these sentences:

1. Steve looked in the mirror and saw . . . .

2. I looked in the mirror and saw . . . .

3. Diana looked in the mirror and saw . . . .

4. You looked in the mirror and saw . . . .

5. The cat looked in the mirror and saw . . . .

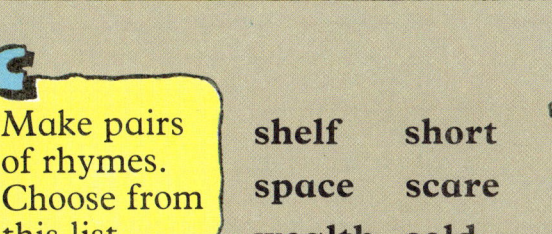

Make pairs of rhymes. Choose from this list.

shelf	short		
space	scare	queen	come
wealth	sold	night	stew

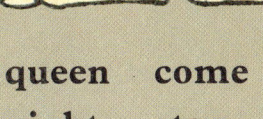

1. some and		6. self and	
2. chew and		7. race and	
3. fort and		8. green and	
4. right and		9. bold and	
5. rare and		10. health and	

A Put the right name on each label on page 8.

picture	window	aeroplane	pyjamas
boots	table	cupboard	radiator
balloon	pillow	football	curtain
shoes	chair	saddle	clothes

 B Make these words:

1. win + dow =
2. cup + board =
3. pill + ow =
4. shall + ow =
5. cur + tain =
6. cer + tain =
7. moun + tain =

8. be + low =
9. pic + ture =
10. na + ture =
11. saxo + phone =
12. tele + phone =
13. Mon + day =
14. Fri + day =

 C Write out the complete words:

d g dow ter	
wink	
win –	
win –	
win – – –	
win – – –	

me pe ble ste	
take	
ta – –	
ta – –	
ta – – –	
ta – – –	

bell   saddle   handlebars
brake   wheel   mudguard
pedal   chain   saddle-bag

A Put the right words on the labels.

B Make pairs of rhymes from this list:

south mouth	

south	prance
paddle	season
reason	dance
muddle	saddle
nurse	puddle
mouth	purse

10

A Choose the words to write under each picture.

two ladies   four countries
six daisies   five flies
ten berries   three puppies

B Write these words in ABC order:

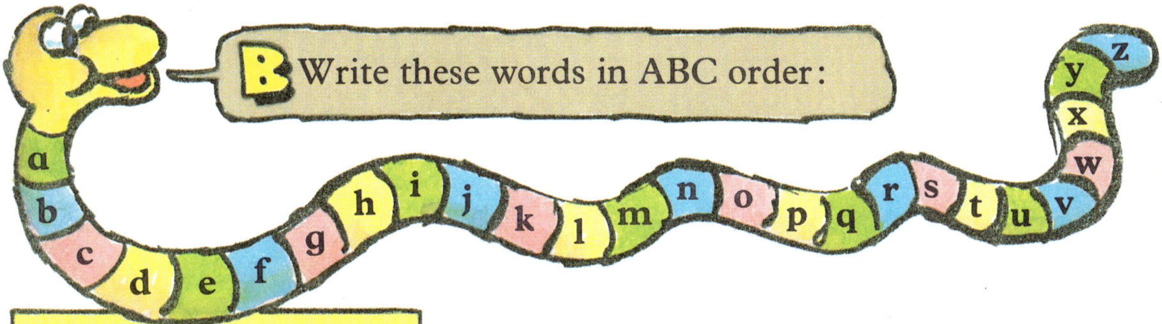

factories	hankies
jellies	armies
duties	cherries
gypsies	babies
enemies	injuries

_____ _____

_____ _____

_____ _____

_____ _____

_____

A Choose the words to write on the picture of the street.

lorry   kerbstone   pavement

house   factories   supermarket

church   gutter   motorbike

basket   shoppers   traffic lights

babies   bicycle   flags

B Write the words with these meanings:

1. _____ something to hold the shopping

2. _____ a shop that sells many different things

3. _____ people who buy things in shops

4. _____ a vehicle to carry heavy loads

5. _____ a path at the side of the street

6. _____ very young children

C Write out the complete words:

b c fl st	
gutter	
– utter	
– utter	
– – utter	
– – utter	

fl sl br del	
light	
– – ight	
– – ight	
– – ight	
– – – ight	

13

A Choose the right words to put with the pictures.

matches	other	plenty
patches	mother	twenty
catches	another	thirty
scratches	brother	body
latches	smother	lucky

B All the words you need are in the list.

1. The opposite of *few*.
2. They fasten doors.
3. She has children.
4. Blessed with luck.
5. Twenty plus ten.
6. 10 + 10.
7. The red picture.

The clowns' trousers are _____

14

What have they just done?

1. Vicky has just . . . . into the pool.

2. John has just . . . . a glass.

3. Mr Lee has just . . . . a tree down.

4. Leela has just . . . .

5. The birds have just . . . . away.

6. Jim has just . . . . on his friend's toe.

7. Liz has just . . . . off her bike.

8. Miss Jones has just . . . . at the lights.

9. Ted has just . . . . to the top of the tree.

chopped   climbed
trodden   dived
stopped   broken
served   flown
fallen

A Choose the right names for the pictures.

onion	butter	pudding
biscuits	chicken	soup
bread	fish	ice-cream
cheese	toast	sausages

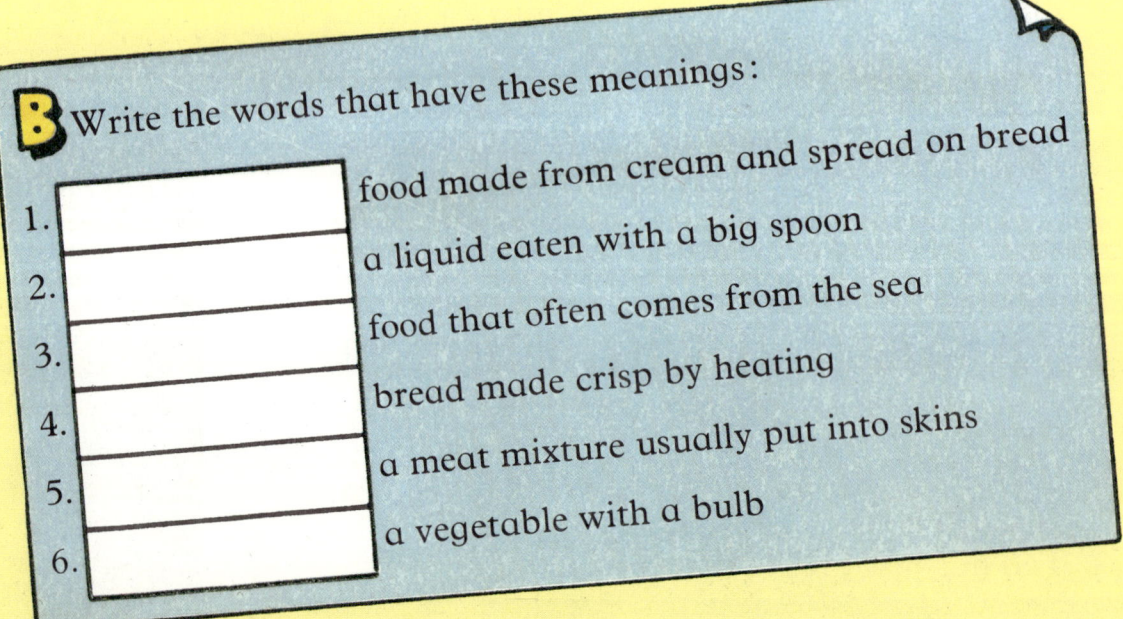

_ _ _ _ _ _ _ _   _ _ _ _ _ _ _ _   _ _ _ _ _ _ _ _   _ _ _ _ _ _ _ _

_ _ _ _ _ _ _ _   _ _ _ _ _ _ _ _   _ _ _ _ _ _ _ _   _ _ _ _ _ _ _ _

B Write the words that have these meanings:

1. _____ food made from cream and spread on bread

2. _____ a liquid eaten with a big spoon

3. _____ food that often comes from the sea

4. _____ bread made crisp by heating

5. _____ a meat mixture usually put into skins

6. _____ a vegetable with a bulb

16

A Put these words in the right lists.

butter	stories	newspapers
milk	cherries	lemonade
water	coffee	strawberries
comics	tea	ice-cream
peaches	poems	notices

You can eat these things.	You can drink these things.	You can read these things.

B Now choose the right words to put under these pictures.

A This is how you make **-ing** words from these words:

| wriggle – wriggling | cuddle – cuddling | scribble – scribbling |

Now make words ending in **-ing** from these:

1. rattle		5. paddle	
2. nibble		6. gobble	
3. juggle		7. struggle	
4. wobble		8. dribble	

B Choose the right words ending in **-ing** to put under these pictures.

_ _ _ _ _ _   _ _ _ _ _ _   _ _ _ _ _ _   _ _ _ _ _ _

 Find on this page a rhyme for each of these words:

1. gobble		4. juggle		7. scribble	
2. saddle		5. puddle		8. smuggle	
3. wobble		6. giggle		9. battle	

18

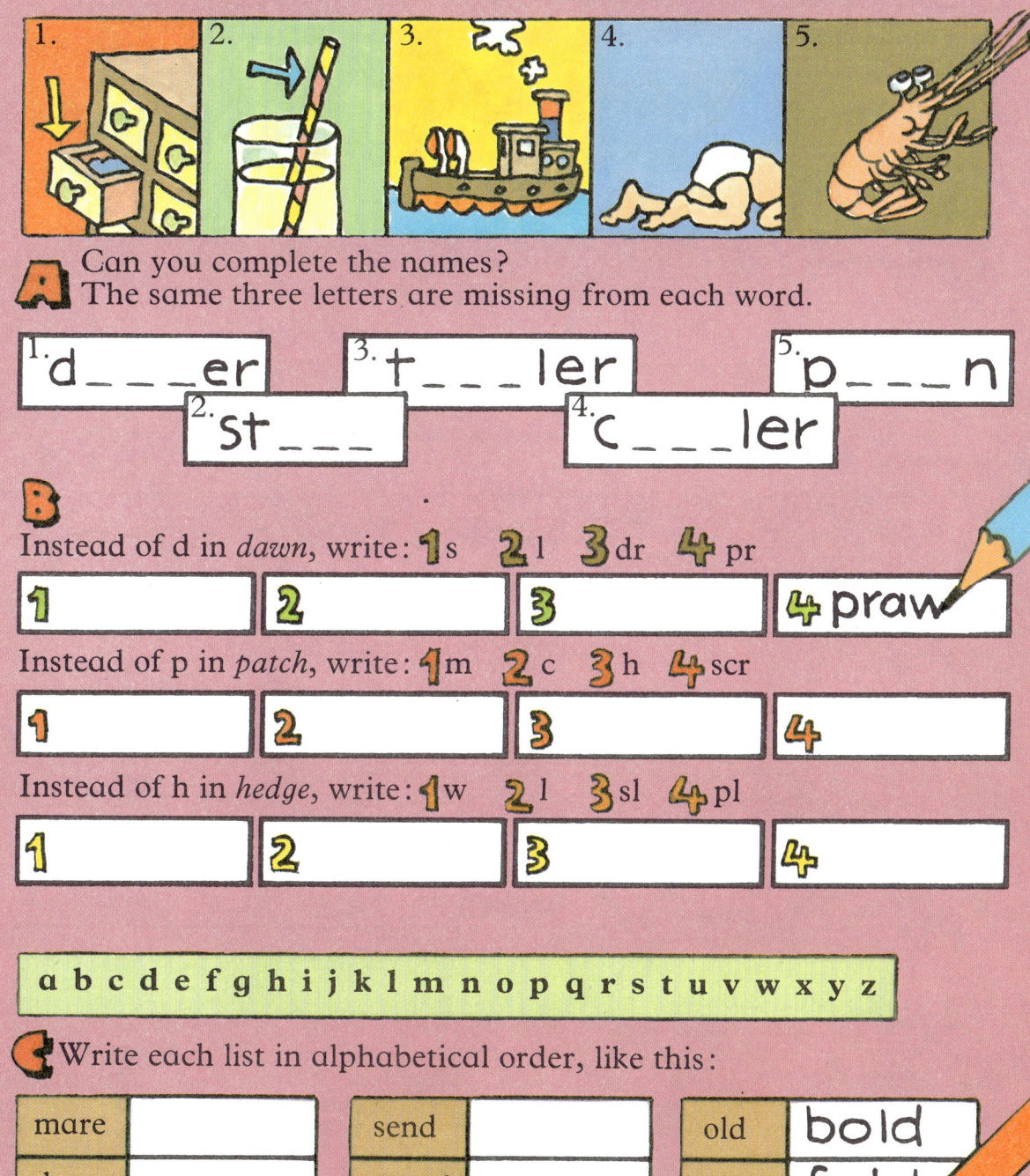

A

Can you complete the names?
The same three letters are missing from each word.

1. d _ _ _ er   3. t _ _ _ ler   5. p _ _ _ n

2. st _ _ _   4. c _ _ _ ler

B

Instead of d in *dawn*, write: **1** s **2** l **3** dr **4** pr

| 1 | 2 | 3 | 4 praw |

Instead of p in *patch*, write: **1** m **2** c **3** h **4** scr

| 1 | 2 | 3 | 4 |

Instead of h in *hedge*, write: **1** w **2** l **3** sl **4** pl

| 1 | 2 | 3 | 4 |

a b c d e f g h i j k l m n o p q r s t u v w x y z

Write each list in alphabetical order, like this:

mare		send		old	bold
dare		mend		fold	fold
rare		bend		scold	gold
scare		trend		gold	
care		lend		bold	

19

Choose the right word to put under each picture.

robbed
scrubbing
stopped

_ _ _ _ _ _ _ _ _ _   _ _ _ _ _ _ _

taught
fighting
caught

_ _ _ _ _ _ _ _ _ _   _ _ _ _ _ _ _

knitted
twisted
broken

_ _ _ _ _ _ _   _ _ _ _ _ _ _

forgotten
forbidden
forgiven

_ _ _ _ _ _ _ _ _ _   _ _ _ _ _ _ _

20

A

Choose the right words to put under the pictures.

dinner rudder fatter
winner shudder chatter
slipper digger swimmer
flipper trigger dagger

_____

_____

_____

_____

_____

B Write the complete words:

k sl fl cl str	
nipper	
– ipper	
– – ipper	
– – ipper	
– – ipper	
– – – ipper	

b ch sc sh cl	
matter	
– atter	
– – atter	
– – atter	
– – atter	
– – atter	

21

Word squares read the same down as across.
Here is one done for you.

	1	2	3	4	5
1	s	c	o	l	d
2	c	a	n	o	e
3	o	n	i	o	n
4	l	o	o	m	s
5	d	e	n	s	e

1. to grumble at, rhyming with *bold*
2. a boat that is paddled
3. a vegetable with a bulb
4. machines for weaving cloth
5. very thick; stupid

Now see if you can solve these word squares:

A

	1	2	3	4	5
1					t
2				e	
3			a		
4		e			
5	t				

1. anything that grows in the ground
2. more low
3. knowing, rhyming with *snare*
4. cheekiness, rhyming with *swerve*
5. large plants with branches

THIS IS LONDON THIS IS ··· ··· IS L

B

	1	2	3	4	5
1	c				
2		p			
3			d		
4				a	
5					e

1. vehicles pulled by horses
2. away from each other
3. sound sent through the air
4. the act of trying out
5. took something belonging to someone else

C

	1	2	3	4	5
1					s
2				a	
3			i		
4		a			
5	s				

1. they catch animals and rhyme with *caps*.
2. to do with the countryside, rhyming with *plura*
3. to get up, rhyming with *wise*
4. thick liquid for sticking
5. not to be awake, rhyming with *deep*

22

Make these words:

1. sun + rise =
2. in + side =
3. out + side =
4. pol + ite =
5. re + cite =
6. es + cape =
7. hope + ful =
8. care + ful =
9. ad + mire =
10. in + quire =
11. pi + rate =

12. nick + name =
13. sur + name =
14. dis + like =
15. ex + plode =
16. six + teen =
17. nine + teen =
18. par + rot =
19. is + land =
20. can + non =
21. con + fuse =
22. a + wake =

B Now find the words above to write on these labels.

23

1. you see better with them
2. night birds
3. a vegetable with a bulb
4. a short pointed weapon
5. flat, thin little cakes
6. a colour
7. hens lay them
8. it pulls things
9. people live in them
10. very cold sweet food
11. you wear them on your feet
12. land with water all round it
13. you ride on it
14. there are five on each foot
15. you hit nails with it
16. you see with them
17. one less than nine
18. ten plus nine
19. a tool for making holes